YELLOW TULIPS

Yellow Tulips

Poems 1968–2011

JAMES FENTON

faber and faber

First published in 2012
by Faber and Faber Ltd
Bloomsbury House
74–77 Great Russell Street
London WC1B 3DA
This paperback edition first published in 2013

Typeset by Refinecatch Ltd, Bungay, Suffolk
Printed in England by T. J. International Ltd, Padstow, Cornwall

The right of James Fenton to be identified as author of
this work has been asserted in accordance with Section 77
of the Copyright, Designs and Patents Act 1988

A CIP record for this book
is available from the British Library

ISBN 978–0571–27383–6

2 4 6 8 10 9 7 5 3 1

Contents

RECENT WORK

from
THE MEMORY OF WAR
and CHILDREN IN EXILE

Wind

This is the wind, the wind in a field of corn.
Great crowds are fleeing from a major disaster
Down the long valleys, the green swaying wadis,
Down through the beautiful catastrophe of wind.

Families, tribes, nations and their livestock
Have heard something, seen something. An expectation
Or misunderstanding has swept over the hilltop
Bending the ear of the hedgerow with stories of fire and sword.

I saw a thousand years pass in two seconds.
Land was lost, languages rose and divided.
This lord went east and found safety.
His brother sought Africa and a dish of aloes.

Centuries, minutes later, one might ask
How the hilt of a sword wandered so far from the smithy.
And somewhere they will sing: 'Like chaff we were borne
In the wind.' This is the wind in a field of corn.

A German Requiem
(to T. J. G. A.)

For as at a great distance of place, that which wee look at, appears dimme, and without distinction of the smaller parts; and as Voyces grow weak, and inarticulate: so also after great distance of time, our imagination of the Past is weak; and wee lose (for example) of Cities wee have seen, many particular Streets; and of Actions, many particular Circumstances. This *decaying sense,* when wee would express the thing it self, (I mean *fancy* it selfe,) wee call *Imagination,* as I said before: But when we would express the *decay,* and signifie that the Sense is fading, old, and past, it is called Memory. So that *Imagination* and *Memory* are but one thing . . .

– Hobbes, *Leviathan*

¶

It is not what they built. It is what they knocked down.
It is not the houses. It is the spaces between the houses.
It is not the streets that exist. It is the streets that no longer exist.
It is not your memories which haunt you.
It is not what you have written down.
It is what you have forgotten, what you must forget.
What you must go on forgetting all your life.
And with any luck oblivion should discover a ritual.
You will find out that you are not alone in the enterprise.
Yesterday the very furniture seemed to reproach you.
Today you take your place in the Widow's Shuttle.

¶

The bus is waiting at the southern gate
To take you to the city of your ancestors
Which stands on the hill opposite, with gleaming pediments,
As vivid as this charming square, your home.
Are you shy? You should be. It is almost like a wedding,
The way you clasp your flowers and give a little tug at your
    veil. Oh,
The hideous bridesmaids, it is natural that you should resent
    them
Just a little, on this first day.
But that will pass, and the cemetery is not far.
Here comes the driver, flicking a toothpick into the gutter,
His tongue still searching between his teeth.
See, he has not noticed you. No one has noticed you.
It will pass, young lady, it will pass.

¶

How comforting it is, once or twice a year,
To get together and forget the old times.
As on those special days, ladies and gentlemen,
When the boiled shirts gather at the graveside
And a leering waistcoat approaches the rostrum.
It is like a solemn pact between the survivors.
The mayor has signed it on behalf of the freemasonry.
The priest has sealed it on behalf of all the rest.
Nothing more need be said, and it is better that way –

¶

The better for the widow, that she should not live in fear of
    surprise,
The better for the young man, that he should move at liberty
    between the armchairs,
The better that these bent figures who flutter among the
    graves
Tending the night-lights and replacing the chrysanthemums
Are not ghosts,
That they shall go home.
The bus is waiting, and on the upper terraces
The workmen are dismantling the houses of the dead.

¶

But when so many had died, so many and at such speed,
There were no cities waiting for the victims.
They unscrewed the name-plates from the shattered
    doorways
And carried them away with the coffins.
So the squares and parks were filled with the eloquence of
    young cemeteries:
The smell of fresh earth, the improvised crosses
And all the impossible directions in brass and enamel.

¶

'Doctor Gliedschirm, skin specialist, surgeries 14–16 hours
or by appointment.'
Professor Sargnagel was buried with four degrees, two
associate memberships
And instructions to tradesmen to use the back entrance.
Your uncle's grave informed you that he lived on the third
floor, left.
You were asked please to ring, and he would come down
in the lift
To which one needed a key . . .

¶

Would come down, would ever come down
With a smile like thin gruel, and never too much to say.
How he shrank through the years.
How you towered over him in the narrow cage.
How he shrinks now . . .

¶

But come. Grief must have its term? Guilt too, then.
And it seems there is no limit to the resourcefulness of
    recollection.
So that a man might say and think:
When the world was at its darkest,
When the black wings passed over the rooftops
(And who can divine His purposes?) even then
There was always, always a fire in this hearth.
You see this cupboard? A priest-hole!
And in that lumber-room whole generations have been
    housed and fed.
Oh, if I were to begin, if I were to begin to tell you
The half, the quarter, a mere smattering of what we went
    through!

¶

His wife nods, and a smile,
Like a breeze with enough strength to carry one dry leaf
Over two pavingstones, passes from chair to chair.
Even the enquirer is charmed.
He forgets to pursue the point.
It is not what he wants to know.
It is what he wants not to know.
It is not what they say.
It is what they do not say.

Cambodia

One man shall smile one day and say goodbye.
Two shall be left, two shall be left to die.

One man shall give his best advice.
Three men shall pay the price.

One man shall live, live to regret.
Four men shall meet the debt.

One man shall wake from terror to his bed.
Five men shall be dead.

One man to five. A million men to one.
And still they die. And still the war goes on.

In a Notebook

There was a river overhung with trees
With wooden houses built along its shallows
From which the morning sun drew up a haze
And the gyrations of the early swallows
Paid no attention to the gentle breeze
Which spoke discreetly from the weeping willows.
There was a jetty by the forest clearing
Where a small boat was tugging at its mooring.

And night still lingered underneath the eaves.
In the dark houseboats families were stirring
And Chinese soup was cooked on charcoal stoves.
Then one by one there came into the clearing
Mothers and daughters bowed beneath their sheaves.
The silent children gathered round me staring
And the shy soldiers setting out for battle
Asked for a cigarette and laughed a little.

From low canoes old men laid out their nets
While on the bank young boys with lines were fishing.
The wicker traps were drawn up by their floats.
The girls stood waist-deep in the river washing
Or tossed the day's rice on enamel plates
And I sat drinking bitter coffee wishing
The tide would turn to bring me to my senses
After the pleasant war and the evasive answers.

There was a river overhung with trees.
The girls stood waist-deep in the river washing,
And night still lingered underneath the eaves
While on the bank young boys with lines were fishing.
Mothers and daughters bowed beneath their sheaves
While I sat drinking bitter coffee wishing –
And the tide turned and brought me to my senses.
The pleasant war brought the unpleasant answers.

The villages are burnt, the cities void;
The morning light has left the river view;
The distant followers have been dismayed;
And I'm afraid, reading this passage now,
That everything I knew has been destroyed
By those whom I admired but never knew;
The laughing soldiers fought to their defeat
And I'm afraid most of my friends are dead.

Dead Soldiers

When His Excellency Prince Norodom Chantaraingsey
Invited me to lunch on the battlefield
I was glad of my white suit for the first time that day.
They lived well, the mad Norodoms, they had style.
The brandy and the soda arrived in crates.
Bricks of ice, tied around with raffia,
Dripped from the orderlies' handlebars.

And I remember the dazzling tablecloth
As the APCs fanned out along the road,
The dishes piled high with frogs' legs,
Pregnant turtles, their eggs boiled in the carapace,
Marsh irises in fish sauce
And inflorescence of a banana salad.

On every bottle, Napoleon Bonaparte
Pleaded for the authenticity of the spirit.
They called the empties Dead Soldiers
And rejoiced to see them pile up at our feet.

Each diner was attended by one of the other ranks
Whirling a table-napkin to keep off the flies.
It was like eating between rows of morris dancers –
Only they didn't kick.

On my left sat the Prince;
On my right, his drunken aide.
The frogs' thighs leapt into the sad purple face
Like fish to the sound of a Chinese flute.
I wanted to talk to the Prince. I wish now
I had collared his aide, who was Saloth Sar's brother.
We treated him as the club bore. He was always
Boasting of his connections, boasting with a head-shake
Or by pronouncing of some doubtful phrase.
And well might he boast. Saloth Sar, for instance,
Was Pol Pot's real name. The APCs
Fired into the sugar palms but met no resistance.

In a diary, I refer to Pol Pot's brother as the Jockey Cap.
A few weeks later, I find him 'in good form
And very skeptical about Chantaraingsey.'
'But one eats well there,' I remark.
'So one should,' says the Jockey Cap:
'The tiger always eats well,
It eats the raw flesh of the deer,
And Chantaraingsey was born in the year of the tiger.
So, did they show you the things they do
With the young refugee girls?'

And he tells me how he will one day give me the gen.
He will tell me how the Prince financed the casino
And how the casino brought Lon Nol to power.
He will tell me this.
He will tell me all these things.
All I must do is drink and listen.

[18]

In those days, I thought that when the game was up
The Prince would be far, far away –
In a limestone faubourg, on the promenade at Nice,
Reduced in circumstances but well enough provided for.
In Paris, he would hardly require his private army.

The Jockey Cap might suffice for café warfare,
And matchboxes for APCs.

But we were always wrong in these predictions.
It was a family war. Whatever happened,
The principals were obliged to attend its issue.
A few were cajoled into leaving, a few were expelled,
And there were villains enough, but none of them
Slipped away with the swag.

For the Prince was fighting Sihanouk, his nephew,
And the Jockey Cap was ranged against his brother
Of whom I remember nothing more
Than an obscure reputation for virtue.
I have been told that the Prince is still fighting
Somewhere in the Cardamoms or the Elephant Mountains.
But I doubt that the Jockey Cap would have survived his
    good connections.

I think the lunches would have done for him –
Either the lunches or the dead soldiers.

Lines for Translation into Any Language

1. I saw that the shanty town had grown over the graves and that the crowd lived among the memorials.

2. It was never very cold – a parachute slung between an angel and an urn afforded shelter for the newcomers.

3. Wooden beds were essential.

4. These people kept their supplies of gasoline in litre bottles, which their children sold at the cemetery gates.

5. That night the city was attacked with rockets.

6. The fire brigade bided its time.

7. The people dug for money beneath their beds, to pay the firemen.

8. The shanty town was destroyed, the cemetery restored.

9. Seeing a plane shot down, not far from the airport, many of the foreign community took fright.

10. The next day, they joined the queues at the gymnasium, asking to leave.

11. When the victorious army arrived, they were welcomed by the fire brigade.

12. This was the only spontaneous demonstration in their favour.

13. Other spontaneous demonstrations in their favour were organised by the victors.

Children in Exile

to J, T, L & S

'What I am is not important, whether I live or die –
  It is the same for me, the same for you.
What we do is important. This is what I have learnt.
  It is not what we are but what we do,'

Says a child in exile, one of a family
  Once happy in its size. Now there are four
Students of calamity, graduates of famine,
  Those whom geography condemns to war,

Who have settled here perforce in a strange country,
  Who are not even certain where they are.
They have learnt much. There is much more to learn.
  Each heart bears a diploma like a scar –

A red seal, always hot, always solid,
  Stamped with the figure of an overseer,
A lethal boy who has learnt to despatch with a mattock,
  Who rules a village with sharp leaves and fear.

From five years of punishment for an offence
  It took America five years to commit
These victim-children have been released on parole.
  They will remember all of it.

They have found out: it is hard to escape from Cambodia,
  Hard to escape the justice of Pol Pot,
When they are called to report in dreams to their tormentors.
  One night is merciful, the next is not.

I hear a child moan in the next room and I see
    The nightmare spread like rain across his face
And his limbs twitch in some vestigial combat
    In some remembered place.

Oh let us not be condemned for what we are.
    It is enough to account for what we do.
Save us from the judge who says: You are your father's son,
    One of your father's crimes – your crime is you.

And save us too from that fatal geography
    Where vengeance is impossible to halt.
And save Cambodia from threatened extinction.
    Let not its history be made its fault.

They feared these woods, feared tigers, snakes and malaria.
    They thought the landscape terrible and wild.
There were ghosts under the beds in the tower room.
    A hooting owl foretold a still-born child.

And how would they survive the snows of Italy?
    For the first weeks, impervious to relief,
They huddled in dark rooms and feared the open air,
    Caught in the tight security of grief.

Fear attacked the skin and made the feet swell
    Though they were bathed in tamarind at night.
Fear would descend like a swarm of flying ants.
    It was impossible to fight.

I saw him once, doubled in pain, scratching his legs,
    This was in Pisa at the Leaning Tower.
We climbed to the next floor and his attackers vanished
    As fast as they had come. He thought some power

Some influence lurked in certain rooms and corners.
    But why was I not suffering as well?
He trod cautiously over the dead in the Campo Santo
    And saw the fading punishments of Hell

And asked whether it is true that the unjust will be tormented
    And whether those who suffer will be saved.
There are so many martyrdoms in the beautiful galleries.
    He was a connoisseur among the graves.

It was the first warm day of the year. The university
    Gossiped in friendly groups around the square.
He envied the students their marvellous education,
    Greedy for school, frantic to be in there.

On the second train he was relaxed and excited.
    For the first time he was returning home,
Pointing his pocket camera at the bright infinity of mountains.
    The winter vines shimmered like chromosomes,

Meaningless to him. The vines grew. The sap returned.
    The land became familiar and green.
The brave bird-life of Italy began planning families.
    It was the season of the selfish gene.

Lovers in cars defied the mad gynaecologist.
   In shady lanes, and later than they should,
They were watching the fireflies' brilliant use of the hyphen
   And the long dash in the darkening wood.

And then they seemed to check the car's suspension
   Or test the maximum back-axle load.
I love this valley, but I often wonder why
   There's always one bend extra in the road.

And what do the dogs defend behind the high wire fences?
   What home needs fury on a running lead?
Why did the Prince require those yellow walls?
   These private landscapes must be wealth indeed.

But you, I am glad to say, are not so fortified.
   The land just peters out behind the house.
(Although, the first time the hunters came blazing through
      the garden,
   Someone screamed at me: 'Get out there. What are you,
      man or mouse?')

When Duschko went mad and ate all those chickens
   It was a cry for help. Now he breaks loose
And visits his fellow guards, and laughs at their misery –
   Unhappy dog! So sensitive to abuse.

He thought there was a quantum of love and attention
   Which now he would be forced to share around
As first three Vietnamese and then four Cambodians
   Trespassed on his ground.

It doesn't work like that. It never has done.
  Love is accommodating. It makes space.
When they were requested to abandon their home in the
    hayloft,
  Even the doves retired with better grace.

They had the tower still, with its commanding eyelets.
  The tiles were fond of them, the sky grew kind.
They watched a new provider spreading corn on the zinc tray
  And didn't mind.

Boat people, foot people, wonky Yankee publishers –
  They'd seen the lot. They knew who slept in which beds.
They swooped down to breakfast after a night on the tiles
  And dropped a benediction on your heads.

And now the school bus comes honking through the valley
  And education litters every room –
Grammars, vocabularies, the Khao-I-Dang hedge dictionary,
  The future perfect, subjunctive moods and gloom.

So many questions in urgent need of answer:
  What is a Pope? What is a proper noun?
Where is Milan? Who won the Second World War?
  How many fluid ounces in a pound?

La Normandie est renommée par ses falaises et ses fromages.
  What are Normandy, cliffs, cheeses and fame?
Too many words on the look-out for too many meanings,
  Too many syllables for the tongue to frame.

[25]

A tiny philosopher climbs onto my knee
    And sinks his loving teeth into my arm.
He has had a good dream. A friendly gun-toting Jesus
    Has spent the night protecting him from harm.

He goes for Technical Lego and significant distinctions.
    Suppose, he says, I have a house and car,
Money and everything, I could lose it all,
    As we lost all our property in the war.

But if I have knowledge, if I know five languages,
    If I have mathematics and the rest,
No one can steal that from me. The difference is:
    No one inherits what I once possessed.

When I die, my education dies with me.
    I cannot leave my knowledge to my son,
Says this boy in exile, and he shrugs and laughs shortly.
    Whoever dreamt of Jesus with a gun?

His brother dreams all night of broken chords
    And all the summer long his broken hand,
Still calloused from hard labour, figures out a prelude.
    Music and maths are what he understands.

These dreams are messages. One of the dead sisters
    Says to the girl: 'Do not be sad for me.
I am alive and in your twin sister's womb
    In California, as you shall see.'

Some time later, the postman brings a letter from America.
   The child bride is expecting her first child.
Months afterwards, a photograph of a little girl.
   Something is reconciled.

Alone in the tower room, the twin keeps up her dancing.
   For the millionth time, Beethoven's 'Für Elise'!
Little Vietnam borrows little Cambodia's toys.
   Mother America is the appeaser.

Pretending to work, I retire to the study
   And find a copy of *The Dyer's Hand*
Where I read: 'An emigrant never knows what he wants,
   Only what he does not want.' I understand

What it is I have seen, how simple and how powerful
   This flight, this negative ambition is
And how a girl in exile can gaze down into an olive grove
   And wonder: 'Is America like this?'

For it is we, not they, who cannot forgive America,
   And it is we who travel, they who flee,
We who may choose exile, they who are forced out,
   Take to the hot roads, take to the sea,

In dangerous camps between facing armies,
   The prey of pirates, raped, plundered or drowned,
In treacherous waters, in single file through the minefields,
   Praying to stave off death till they are found,

Begging for sponsors, begging for a Third Country,
  Begging America to take them in –
It is they, it is they who put everything in hazard.
  What we do decides whether they sink or swim.

Do they know what they want? They know what they do
    not want.
  Better the owl before dawn than the devil by day.
Better strange food than famine, hard speech than mad
    labour.
  Better this quietness than that dismay.

Better ghosts under the bed than to sleep in the paddy.
  Better this frost, this blizzard than that sky.
Better a concert pianist than a corpse, an engineer than
    a shadow.
  Better to dance under the fresco than to die.

Better a new god with bleeding hands and feet,
  Better the painted tortures of the blest
Than the sharp leaf at the throat, the raised mattock
  And all the rest.

My dear American friends, I can't say how much it means
    to me
  To see this little family unfurl,
To see them relax and learn, and learn about happiness,
  The mother growing strong, the boys adept, the girl

Confident in your care. They can never forget the past.
Let them remember, but let them not fear.
Let them find their future is delightfully accomplished
And find perhaps America is here.

Let them come to the crest of the road when the morning
is fine
With Florence spread like honey on the plain,
Let them walk through the ghostless woods, let the guns
be silent,
The tiger never catch their eye again.

They are thriving I see. I hope they always thrive
Whether in Italy, England or France.
Let them dream as they wish to dream. Let them dream

Of Jesus, America, maths, Lego, music and dance.

A Vacant Possession

In a short time we shall have cleared the gazebo.
Look how you can scrape the weeds from the paving stones
With a single motion of the foot. Paths lead down
Past formal lawns, orchards, notional guinea-fowl
To where the house is entirely obscured from view.

And there are gravel drives beneath the elm-tree walks
On whose aquarium green the changing weather
Casts no shadow. Urns pour their flowers out beside
A weathered Atlas with the whole world to support.
Look, it is now night and there are lights in the trees.

The difficult guest is questioning his rival.
He is pacing up and down while she leans against
A mossy water-butt in which, could we see them,
Innumerable forms of life are uncurving.
She is bravely not being hurt by his manner

Of which they have warned her. He taps his cigarette
And brusquely changed the subject. He remembers
Something said earlier which she did not really mean.
Nonsense – she did mean it. Now he is satisfied.
She has bitten the quick of her thumb-nail, which bleeds.

What shall we do the next day? The valley alters.
You set out from the village and the road turns around,
So that, in an hour, behind a clump of oak-trees,
With a long whitewashed wall and a low red-tiled roof
Peaceful, unevenly they appear again.

The square, the café seats, the doorways are empty
And the long grey balconies stretch out on all sides.
Time for an interlude, evening in the country,
With distant cowbells providing the angelus.
But we are interrupted by the latest post.

'Of course you will never understand. How could you?
You had everything. Everything always went well
For you. If there was a court at which I could sue you
I should take you for every memory you have.
No doubt you are insured against your murdered friends.'

Or: 'We see very little of Hester these days.
Why don't you come home? Your room is as you left it.
I went in yesterday, looking for notepaper,
And – do you know – the noose is still over the bed!
Archie says he will bring it out to you this summer.'

On warm spring afternoons, seated in the orchard,
The smocked, serious students develop grave doubts
About Pascal's wager. Monsieur le Curé stays
Chatting till midnight over the porcelain stove.
The last of his nine proofs lies smouldering in the grate.

I have set up my desk in an old dressing-room
So that the shadow of the fig-tree will be cast
On this page. At night, on the mountain opposite,
The beam of approaching cars is seen in the sky.
And now a slamming door and voices in the hall,

Scraping suitcases and laughter. Shall I go down?
I hear my name called, peer over the bannister
And remember something I left in my bedroom.
What can it have been? The window is wide open.
The curtains move. The light sways. The cold sets in.

A Staffordshire Murderer

Every fear is a desire. Every desire is fear.
The cigarettes are burning under the trees
Where the Staffordshire murderers wait for their
    accomplices
And victims. Every victim is an accomplice.

It takes a lifetime to stroll to the carpark
Stopping at the footbridge for reassurance,
Looking down at the stream, observing
(With one eye) the mallard's diagonal progress
    backwards.

You could cut and run, now. It is not too late.
But your fear is like a long-case clock
In the last whirring second before the hour,
The hammer drawn back, the heart ready to chime.

Fear turns the ignition. The van is unlocked.
You may learn now what you ought to know:
That every journey begins with a death,
That the suicide travels alone, that the murderer
    needs company.

And the Staffordshire murderers, nervous though
    they are,
Are masters of the conciliatory smile.
A cigarette? A tablet in a tin?
Would you care for a boiled sweet, from the
    famous poisoner

Of Rugeley? These are his own brand.
He has never had any complaints.
He speaks of his victims as a sexual braggart
With a tradesman's emphasis on the word 'satisfaction'.

You are flattered as never before. He appreciates
So much, the little things – your willingness for instance
To bequeath your body at once to his experiments.
He sees the point of you as no one else does.

Large parts of Staffordshire have been undermined.
The trees are in it up to their necks. Fish
Nest in their branches. In one of the Five Towns
An ornamental pond disappeared overnight

Dragging the ducks down with it, down to the old seams
With a sound as of a gigantic bath running out,
Which is in turn the sound of ducks in distress.
Thus History murders mallards, while we hear nothing

Or what we hear we do not understand.
It is heard as the tramp's rage in the crowded precinct:
'Woe to the bloody city of Lichfield.'
It is lost in the enthusiasm of the windows

From which we are offered on the easiest terms
Five times over in colour and once in monochrome
The first reprisals after the drill-sergeant's coup.
How speedily the murder detail makes its way

Along the green beach, past the pink breakers,
And binds the whole cabinet to the oil-drums,
Where death is a preoccupied tossing of the head,
Where no decorative cloud lingers at the gun's mouth.

At the Dame's School dust gathers on the highwayman,
On Sankey and Moody, Wesley and Fox,
On the snoring churchwarden, on Palmer the Poisoner
And Palmer's house and Stanfield Hall.

The brilliant moss has been chipped from the Red Barn.
They say that Cromwell played ping-pong with the
      cathedral.
We train roses over the arches. In the Minster Pool
Crayfish live under carved stones. Every spring

The rats pick off the young mallards and
The good weather brings out the murderers
By the Floral Clock, by the footbridge,
The pottery murderers in jackets of prussian blue.

'Alack, George, where are thy shoes?'
He lifted up his head and espied the three
Steeple-house spires, and they struck at his life.
And he went by his eye over hedge and ditch

And no one laid hands on him, and he went
Thus crying through the streets, where there seemed
To be a channel of blood running through the streets,
And the market-place appeared like a pool of blood.

For this field of corpses was Lichfield
Where a thousand Christian Britons fell
In Diocletian's day, and 'much could I write
Of the sense that I had of the blood –'

That winter Friday. Today it is hot.
The cowparsley is so high that the van cannot be seen
From the road. The bubbles rise in the warm canal.
Below the lock-gates you can hear mallards.

A coot hurries along the tow-path, like a Queen's
    Messenger.
On the heli-pad, an arrival in blue livery
Sends the water-boatmen off on urgent business.
News of a defeat. Keep calm. The cathedral chimes.

The house by the bridge is the house in your dream.
It stares through new frames, unwonted spectacles,
And the paint, you can tell, has been weeping.
In the yard, five striped oildrums. Flowers in a tyre.

This is where the murderer works. But it is Sunday.
Tomorrow's bank holiday will allow the bricks to set.
You see? he has thought of everything. He shows you
The snug little cavity he calls 'your future home'.

And 'Do you know,' he remarks, 'I have been counting
  my victims.
Nine hundred and ninety nine, the Number of the Beast!
That makes you . . .' But he sees he has overstepped
  the mark:
'I'm sorry, but you cannot seriously have thought you
  were the first?'

A thousand preachers, a thousand poisoners,
A thousand martyrs, a thousand murderers –
Surely these preachers are poisoners, these martyrs
  murderers?
Surely this is all a gigantic mistake?

But there has been no mistake. God and the weather
  are glorious.
You have come as an anchorite to kneel at your funeral.
Kneel then and pray. The blade flashes a smile.
This is your new life. This murder is yours.

The Pitt-Rivers Museum, Oxford

Is shut
22 hours a day and all day Sunday
And should not be confused
With its academic brother, full of fossils
And skeletons of bearded seals. Take
Your heart in your hand and go; it does not sport
Any of Ruskin's hothouse Venetian
And resembles rather, with its dusty girders,
A vast gymnasium or barracks – though
The resemblance ends where

Entering
You will find yourself in a climate of nut castanets,
A musical whip
From the Torres Straits, from Mirzapur a sistrum
Called Jumka, 'used by aboriginal
Tribes to attract small game
On dark nights', a mute violin,
Whistling arrows, coolie cigarettes
And a mask of Saagga, the Devil Doctor,
The eyelids worked by strings.

Outside,
All around you, there are students researching
With a soft electronic
Hum, but here, where heels clang
On iron grates, voices are at best
Disrespectful: 'Please sir, where's the withered
Hand?' For teachers the thesis is salutary
And simple, a hierarchy of progress culminating
In the Entrance Hall, but children are naturally
Unaware of and unimpressed by this.

Encountering
'A jay's feather worn as a charm
In Buckinghamshire, Stone',
We cannot either feel that we have come
Far or in any particular direction.
Item. A dowser's twig, used by Webb
For locating the spring, 'an excellent one',
For Lord Pembroke's waterworks at Dinton
Village. 'The violent twisting is shown
On both limbs of the fork.'

Yes
You have come upon the fabled lands where myths
Go when they die,
But some, especially the Brummagem capitalist
Juju, have arrived prematurely. Idols
Cast there and sold to tribes for a huge
Price for human sacrifice do
(Though slightly hidden) actually exist
And we do well to bring large parties
Of schoolchildren here to find them.

Outdated
Though the cultural anthropological system be
The lonely and unpopular
Might find the landscapes of their childhood marked out
Here, in the chaotic piles of souvenirs.
The claw of a condor, the jaw-bone of a dolphin,
These cleave the sky and the waves but they
Would trace from their windowseats the storm petrel's path
From Lindness or Naze to the North Cape,
Sheltered in the trough of the wave.

For the solitary,
The velveted only child who wrestled
With eagles for their feathers
And the young girl on the hill, who heard
The din on the causeway and saw the large
Hound with the strange pretercanine eyes
Herald the approach of her turbulent lover,
This boxroom of the forgotten or hardly possible
Is laid with the snares of privacy and fiction
And the dangerous third wish.

Beware.
You are entering the climate of a foreign logic
And are cursed by the hair
Of a witch, earth from the grave of a man
Killed by a tiger and a woman who died
In childbirth, 2 leaves from the tree
Azumü, which withers quickly, a nettle-leaf,
A leaf from the swiftly deciduous 'Flame of the
Forest' and a piece of a giant taro,
A strong irritant if eaten.

Go
As a historian of ideas or a sex-offender,
For the primitive art,
As a dusty semiologist, equipped to unravel
The seven components of that witch's curse
Or the syntax of the mutilated teeth. Go
In groups to giggle at curious finds.
But do not step into the kingdom of your promises
To yourself, like a child entering the forbidden
Woods of his lonely playtime:

All day,
Watching the groundsman breaking the ice
From the stone trough,
The sun slanting across the lawns, the grass
Thawing, the stable-boy blowing on his fingers,
He had known what tortures the savages had prepared
For him there, as he calmly pushed open the gate
And entered the wood near the placard: 'TAKE NOTICE
MEN-TRAPS AND SPRING-GUNS ARE SET ON THESE PREMISES.'
For his father had protected his good estate.

God, A Poem

A nasty surprise in a sandwich,
A drawing-pin caught in your sock,
The limpest of shakes from a hand which
You'd thought would be firm as a rock,

A serious mistake in a nightie,
A grave disappointment all round
Is all that you'll get from th'Almighty,
Is all that you'll get underground.

Oh he *said*: 'If you lay off the crumpet
I'll see you alright in the end.
Just hang on until the last trumpet.
Have faith in me, chum – I'm your friend.'

But if you remind him, he'll tell you:
'I'm sorry, I must have been pissed –
Though your name rings a sort of a bell. You
Should have guessed that I do not exist.

'I didn't exist at Creation,
I didn't exist at the Flood,
And I won't be around for Salvation
To sort out the sheep from the cud –

'Or whatever the phrase is. The fact is
In soteriological terms
I'm a crude existential malpractice
And you are a diet of worms.

'You're a nasty surprise in a sandwich.
You're a drawing-pin caught in my sock.
You're the limpest of shakes from a hand which
I'd have thought would be firm as a rock,

'You're a serious mistake in a nightie,
You're a grave disappointment all round –
That's all that you are,' says th'Almighty,
'And that's all that you'll be underground.'

Nothing

I take a jewel from a junk-shop tray
And wish I had a love to buy it for.
Nothing I choose will make you turn my way.
Nothing I give will make you love me more.

I know that I've embarrassed you too long
And I'm ashamed to linger at your door.
Whatever I embark on will be wrong.
Nothing I do will make you love me more.

I cannot work. I cannot read or write.
How can I frame a letter to implore.
Eloquence is a lie. The truth is trite.
Nothing I say will make you love me more.

So I replace the jewel in the tray
And laughingly pretend I'm far too poor.
Nothing I give, nothing I do or say,
Nothing I am will make you love me more.

The Song That Sounds Like This
To Philip Dennis

Have you not heard the song
The Song That Sounds Like This
When skies are overcast and looks grow long
And Radio Three
Is all your tea-time company.
The last of the first infusion comes so strong
The apostle spoon wakes up
And clambers from the cup.
Have you not heard it? Have you not heard
the song –
Antithesis of bliss –
The Song That Sounds Like This!

Have you not heard them sing
Those songs that sound like these
When yearning for the telephone to ring.
The sky is dark.
The dogs have gone to foul the park.
The first of the next infusion tastes like string.
Oh melancholy sound.
All the apostle spoons have drowned.
Have you not heard them, have you not heard
them sing –
No more, oh please,
Oh give us no more songs,
Oh give us no more Songs That Sound Like These!

The Skip

I took my life and threw it on the skip,
Reckoning the next-door neighbours wouldn't mind
If my life hitched a lift to the council tip
With their dry rot and rubble. What you find

With skips is – the whole community joins in.
Old mattresses appear, doors kind of drift
Along with all that won't fit in the bin
And what the bin-men can't be fished to shift.

I threw away my life, and there it lay
And grew quite sodden. 'What a dreadful shame,'
Clucked some old bag and sucked her teeth: 'The way
The young these days . . . no values . . . me, I blame . . .'

But I blamed no one. Quality control
Had loused it up, and that was that. 'Nough said.
I couldn't stick at home. I took a stroll
And passed the skip, and left my life for dead.

Without my life, the beer was just as foul,
The landlord still as filthy as his wife,
The chicken in the basket was an owl,
And no one said: 'Ee, Jim-lad, whur's thee life?'

Well, I got back that night the worse for wear,
But still just capable of single vision;
Looked in the skip; my life – it wasn't there!
Some bugger'd nicked it – *without* my permission.

Okay, so I got angry and began
To shout, and woke the street. Okay. *Okay!*
And I was sick all down the neighbour's van.
And I disgraced myself on the par-*kay*.

And then . . . you know how if you've had a few
You'll wake at dawn, all healthy, like sea breezes,
Raring to go, and thinking: 'Clever you!
You've got away with it.' And then, oh Jesus,

It hits you. Well, that morning, just at six
I woke, got up and looked down at the skip.
There lay my life, still sodden, on the bricks;
There lay my poor old life, arse over tip.

Or was it mine? Still dressed, I went downstairs
And took a long cool look. The truth was dawning.
Someone had just exchanged my life for theirs.
Poor fool, I thought – I should have left a warning.

Some bastard saw my life and thought it nicer
Than what he had. Yet what he'd had seemed fine.
He'd never caught his fingers in the slicer
The way I'd managed in that life of mine.

His life lay glistening in the rain, neglected,
Yet still a decent, an authentic life.
Some people I can think of, I reflected
Would take that thing as soon as you'd say Knife.

It seemed a shame to miss a chance like that.
I brought the life in, dried it by the stove.
It looked so fetching, stretched out on the mat.
I tried it on. It fitted, like a glove.

And now, when some local bat drops off the twig
And new folk take the house, and pull up floors
And knock down walls and hire some kind of big
Container (say, a skip) for their old doors,

I'll watch it like a hawk, and every day
I'll make at least – oh – half a dozen trips.
I've furnished an existence in that way.
You'd not believe the things you find on skips.

from
OUT OF DANGER

Beauty, Danger and Dismay

Beauty, danger and dismay
Met me on the public way.
Whichever I chose, I chose dismay.

Out of Danger

Heart be kind and sign the release
As the trees their loss approve.
Learn as leaves must learn to fall
Out of danger, out of love.

What belongs to frost and thaw
Sullen winter will not harm.
What belongs to wind and rain
Is out of danger from the storm.

Jealous passion, cruel need
Betray the heart they feed upon.
But what belongs to earth and death
Is out of danger from the sun.

I was cruel, I was wrong –
Hard to say and hard to know.
You do not belong to me.
You are out of danger now –

Out of danger from the wind,
Out of danger from the wave,
Out of danger from the heart
Falling, falling out of love.

Serious

Awake, alert,
Suddenly serious in love,
You're a surprise.
I've known you long enough –
Now I can hardly meet your eyes.

It's not that I'm
Embarrassed or ashamed.
You've changed the rules
The way I'd hoped they'd change
Before I thought: hopes are for fools.

Let me walk with you.
I've got the newspapers to fetch.
I think you know
I think you have the edge
But I feel cheerful even so.

That's why I laughed.
That's why I went and kicked that stone.
I'm serious!
That's why I cartwheeled home.
This should mean something. Yes, it does.

The Ideal

This is where I came from.
I passed this way.
This should not be shameful
Or hard to say.

A self is a self.
It is not a screen.
A person should respect
What he has been.

This is my past
Which I shall not discard.
This is the ideal.
This is hard.

Hinterhof

Stay near to me and I'll stay near to you –
As near as you are dear to me will do,
  Near as the rainbow to the rain,
  The west wind to the windowpane,
As fire to the hearth, as dawn to dew.

Stay true to me and I'll stay true to you –
As true as you are new to me will do,
  New as the rainbow in the spray,
  Utterly new in every way,
New in the way that what you say is true.

Stay near to me, stay true to me. I'll stay
As near, as true to you as heart could pray.
  Heart never hoped that one might be
  Half of the things you are to me –
The dawn, the fire, the rainbow and the day.

The Possibility

The lizard on the wall, engrossed,
The sudden silence from the wood
Are telling me that I have lost
The possibility of good.

I know this flower is beautiful
And yesterday it seemed to be.
It opened like a crimson hand.
It was not beautiful to me.

I know that work is beautiful.
It is a boon. It is a good.
Unless my working were a way
Of squandering my solitude.

And solitude was beautiful
When I was sure that I was strong.
I thought it was a medium
In which to grow, but I was wrong.

The jays are swearing in the wood.
The lizard moves with ugly speed.
The flower closes like a fist.
The possibility recedes.

The Mistake

With the mistake your life goes in reverse.
Now you can see exactly what you did
Wrong yesterday and wrong the day before
And each mistake leads back to something worse

And every nuance of your hypocrisy
Towards yourself, and every excuse
Stands solidly on the perspective lines
And there is perfect visibility.

What an enlightenment. The colonnade
Rolls past on either side. You needn't move.
The statues of your errors brush your sleeve.
You watch the tale turn back – and you're dismayed.

And this dismay at this, this big mistake
Is made worse by the sight of all those who
Knew all along where these mistakes would lead –
Those frozen friends who watched the crisis break.

Why didn't they *say*? Oh, but they did indeed –
Said with a murmur when the time was wrong
Or by a mild refusal to assent
Or told you plainly but you would not heed.

Yes, you can hear them now. It hurts. It's worse
Than any sneer from any enemy.
Take this dismay. Lay claim to this mistake.
Look straight along the lines of this reverse.

I'll Explain

It's something you say at your peril.
It's something you shouldn't contain.
It's a truth for the dark and a pillow.
Turn out the light and I'll explain.

It's the obvious truth of the morning
Bitten back as the sun turns to rain,
To the rain, to the dark, to the pillow.
Turn out the light and I'll explain.

>   It's what I was hoping to tell you.
>   It's what I was hoping you'd guess.
>   It's what I was hoping you *wouldn't* guess
>   Or you wouldn't mind.
>   It's a kind
>   Of hopelessness.

It's the hope that you hope at your peril.
It's the hope that you fear to attain.
It's the obvious truth of the evening.
Turn out the light and I'll explain.

In Paris with You

Don't talk to me of love. I've had an earful
And I get tearful when I've downed a drink or two.
I'm one of your talking wounded.
I'm a hostage. I'm marooned.
But I'm in Paris with you.

Yes I'm angry at the way I've been bamboozled
And resentful at the mess that I've been through.
I admit I'm on the rebound
And I don't care where are *we* bound.
I'm in Paris with you.

Do you mind if we do *not* go to the Louvre,
If we say sod off to sodding Notre Dame,
If we skip the Champs Elysées
And remain here in this sleazy
Old hotel room
Doing this and that
To what and whom
Learning who you are,
Learning what I am.

Don't talk to me of love. Let's talk of Paris,
The little bit of Paris in our view.
There's that crack across the ceiling
And the hotel walls are peeling
And I'm in Paris with you.

Don't talk to me of love. Let's talk of Paris.
I'm in Paris with the slightest thing you do.
I'm in Paris with your eyes, your mouth,
I'm in Paris with . . . all points south.
Am I embarrassing you?
I'm in Paris with you.

The Milkfish Gatherers
to G.L.

The sea sounds insincere
Giving and taking with one hand.
It stopped a river here last month
Filling its mouth with sand.

They drag the shallows for the milkfish fry –
Two eyes on a glass noodle, nothing more.
Roused by his vigilant young wife
The drowsy stevedore

Comes running barefoot past the swamp
To meet a load of wood.
The yellow peaked cap, the patched pink shorts
Seem to be all his worldly goods.

The nipa booths along the coast
Protect the milkfish gatherers' rights.
Nothing goes unobserved. My good custodian
Sprawls in the deckchair through the night.

Take care, he says, take care –
Not everybody is a friend.
And so he makes my life more private still –
A privacy on which he will attend.

But the dogs are sly with the garbage
And the cats ruthless, even with sliced bread,
As the terns are ruthless among the shoals.
Men watch the terns, then give the boat its head

Dragging a wide arc through the blue,
Trailing their lines,
Cutting the engine out
At the first sign.

A hundred feet away
Something of value struggles not to die.
It will sell for a dollar a kilo.
It weighs two kilos on the line – a prize.

And the hull fills with a fortune
And the improbable colours of the sea
But the spine lives when the brain dies
In a convulsive misery.

Rummagers of inlets, scourers of the deep,
Dynamite men, their bottles crammed with wicks,
They named the sea's inhabitants with style –
The slapped vagina fish, the horse's dick.

Polillo 'melts' means it is far away –
The smoking island plumed from slash and burn.
And from its shore, busy with hermit crabs,
Look to Luzon. Infanta melts in turn.

The setting sun behind the Sierra Madre
Projects a sharp blue line across the sky
And in the eastern glow beyond Polillo
It looks as if another sun might rise –

As if there were no night,
Only a brother evening and a dawn.
No night! No death! How could these people live?
How could the pressure lanterns lure the prawns?

Nothing of value has arrived all day –
No timber, no rattan. Now after dark,
The news comes from the sea. They crowd the beach
And prime a lantern, waiting for the shark.

The young receive the gills, which they will cook.
The massive liver wallows on the shore
And the shark's teeth look like a row of sharks
Advancing along a jaw.

Alone again by spirit light
I notice something happening on a post.
Something has burst its skin and now it hangs,
Hangs for dear life onto its fine brown ghost.

Clinging exhausted to its former self,
Its head flung back as if to watch the moon,
The blue-green veins pulsing along its wings,
The thing unwraps itself, but falls too soon.

The ants are tiny and their work is swift –
The insect-shark is washed up on their land –
While the sea sounds insincere,
Giving and taking with one hand.

At dawn along the seashore come
The milkfish gatherers, human fry.
A white polythene bowl
Is what you need to sort the milkfish by.

For a hatched fish is a pair of eyes –
There is nothing more to see.
But the spine lives when the brain dies
In a convulsive misery.

Jerusalem

I

Stone cries to stone,
Heart to heart, heart to stone,
And the interrogation will not die
For there is no eternal city
And there is no pity
And there is nothing underneath the sky
No rainbow and no guarantee –
There is no covenant between your God and me.

II

It is superb in the air.
Suffering is everywhere
And each man wears his suffering like a skin.
My history is proud.
Mine is not allowed.
This is the cistern where all wars begin,
The laughter from the armoured car.
This is the man who won't believe you're what you are.

III

This is your fault.
This is a crusader vault.
The Brook of Kidron flows from Mea She'arim.
I will pray for you.
I will tell you what to do.
I'll stone you. I shall break your every limb.
Oh I am not afraid of you
But maybe I should fear the things you make me do.

IV

This is not Golgotha.
This is the Holy Sepulchre,
The Emperor Hadrian's temple to a love
Which he did not much share.
Golgotha could be anywhere.
Jerusalem itself is on the move.
It leaps and leaps from hill to hill
And as it makes its way it also makes its will.

V

The city was sacked.
Jordan was driven back.
The pious Christians burned the Jews alive.
This is a minaret.
I'm not finished yet.
We're waiting for reinforcements to arrive.
What was your mother's real name?
Would it be safe today to go to Bethlehem?

VI

This is the Garden Tomb.
No, *this* is the Garden Tomb.
I'm an Armenian. I am a Copt.
This is Utopia.
I came here from Ethiopia.
This hole is where the flying carpet dropped
The Prophet off to pray one night
And from here one hour later he resumed his flight.

VII

Who packed your bag?
I packed my bag.
Where was your uncle's mother's sister born?
Have you ever met an Arab?
Yes I am a scarab.
I am a worm. I am a thing of scorn.
I cry Impure from street to street
And see my degradation in the eyes I meet.

VIII

I am your enemy.
This is Gethsemane.
The broken graves look to the Temple Mount.
Tell me now, tell me when
When shall we all rise again?
Shall I be first in the great body count?
When shall the tribes be gathered in?
When, tell me, when shall the Last Things begin?

IX

You are in error.
This is terror.
This is your banishment. This land is mine.
This is what you earn.
This is the Law of No Return.
This is the sour dough, this the sweet wine.
This is my history, this my race
And this unhappy man threw acid in my face.

Stone cries to stone,
   Heart to heart, heart to stone.
These are the warrior archaeologists.
   This is us and that is them.
   This is Jerusalem.
These are the dying men with tattooed wrists.
   Do this and I'll destroy your home.
I have destroyed your home. You have destroyed my home.

December 1988

For Andrew Wood

What would the dead want from us
Watching from their cave?
Would they have us forever howling?
Would they have us rave
Or disfigure ourselves, or be strangled
Like some ancient emperor's slave?

None of my dead friends were emperors
With such exorbitant tastes
And none of them were so vengeful
As to have all their friends waste
Waste quite away in sorrow
Disfigured and defaced.

I think the dead would want us
To weep for what *they* have lost.
I think that our luck in continuing
Is what would affect them most.
But time would find them generous
And less self-engrossed.

And time would find them generous
As they used to be
And what else would they want from us
But an honoured place in our memory,
A favourite room, a hallowed chair,
Privilege and celebrity?

And so the dead might cease to grieve
And we might make amends
And there might be a pact between
Dead friends and living friends.
What our dead friends would want from us
Would be such living friends.

Out of the East

Out of the South came Famine.
Out of the West came Strife.
Out of the North came a storm cone
And out of the East came a warrior wind
And it struck you like a knife.
Out of the East there shone a sun
As the blood rose on the day
And it shone on the work of the warrior wind
And it shone on the heart
And it shone on the soul
And they called the sun – Dismay.

And it's a far cry from the jungle
To the city of Phnom Penh
And many try
And many die
Before they can see their homes again
And it's a far cry from the paddy track
To the palace of the King
And many go
Before they know
It's a far cry.
It's a war cry.
Cry for the war that can do this thing.

A foreign soldier came to me
And he gave me a gun
And he predicted victory
Before the year was done.

He taught me how to kill a man.
He taught me how to try.
But he forgot to say to me
How an honest man should die.

He taught me how to kill a man
Who was my enemy
But never how to kill a man
Who'd been a friend to me.

You fought the way a hero fights –
You had no head for fear
My friend, but you are wounded now
And I'm not allowed to leave you here

Alive.

Out of the East came Anger
And it walked a dusty road
And it stopped when it came to a river bank
And it pitched a camp
And it gazed across
To where the city stood
When
Out of the West came thunder
But it came without a sound
For it came at the speed of the warrior wind
And it fell on the heart
And it fell on the soul
And it shook the battleground

And it's a far cry from the cockpit
To the foxhole in the clay
And we were a
Coordinate
In a foreign land
Far away
And it's a far cry from the paddy track
To the palace of the King
And many try
And they ask why
It's a far cry.
It's a war cry.
Cry for the war that can do this thing.

Next year the army came for me
And I was sick and thin
And they put a weapon in our hands
And they told us we would win

And they feasted us for seven days
And they slaughtered a hundred cattle
And we sang our songs of victory
And the glory of the battle

And they sent us down the dusty roads
In the stillness of the night
And when the city heard from us
It burst in a flower of light.

The tracer bullets found us out.
The guns were never wrong
And the gunship said Regret Regret
The words of your victory song.

Out of the North came an army
And it was clad in black
And out of the South came a gun crew
With a hundred shells
And a howitzer
And we walked in black along the paddy track
When
Out of the West came napalm
And it tumbled from the blue
And it spread at the speed of the warrior wind
And it clung to the heart
And it clung to the soul
As napalm is designed to do

And it's a far cry from the fireside
To the fire that finds you there
In the foxhole
By the temple gate
The fire that finds you everywhere
And it's a far cry from the paddy track
To the palace of the King
And many try
And they ask why
It's a far cry.
It's a war cry.
Cry for the war that can do this thing.

My third year in the army
I was sixteen years old
And I had learnt enough, my friend,
To believe what I was told

And I was told that we would take
The city of Phnom Penh
And they slaughtered all the cows we had
And they feasted us again

And at last we were given river mines
And we blocked the great Mekong
And now we trained our rockets on
The landing-strip at Pochentong.

The city lay within our grasp.
We only had to wait.
We only had to hold the line
By the foxhole, by the temple gate

When
Out of the West came clusterbombs
And they burst in a hundred shards
And every shard was a new bomb
And it burst again
Upon our men
As they gasped for breath in the temple yard.
Out of the West came a new bomb
And it sucked away the air
And it sucked at the heart
And it sucked at the soul
And it found a lot of children there

[77]

And it's a far cry from the temple yard
To the map of the general staff
From the grease pen to the gasping men
To the wind that blows the soul like chaff
And it's a far cry from the paddy track
To the palace of the King
And many go
Before they know
It's a far cry.
It's a war cry.
Cry for the war that has done this thing.

A foreign soldier came to me
And he gave me a gun
And the liar spoke of victory
Before the year was done.

What would I want with victory
In the city of Phnom Penh?
Punish the city! Punish the people!
What would I want but punishment?

We have brought the King home to his palace.
We shall leave him there to weep
And we'll go back along the paddy track
For we have promises to keep.

For the promise made in the foxhole,
For the oath in the temple yard,
For the friend I killed on the battlefield
I shall make that punishment hard.

Out of the South came Famine.
Out of the West came Strife.
Out of the North came a storm cone
And out of the East came a warrior wind
And it struck you like a knife.
Out of the East there shone a sun
As the blood rose on the day
And it shone on the work of the warrior wind
And it shone on the heart
And it shone on the soul
And they called the sun Dismay, my friend,
They called the sun – Dismay.

Blood and Lead

Listen to what they did.
Don't listen to what they said.
What was written in blood
Has been set up in lead.

Lead tears the heart.
Lead tears the brain.
What was written in blood
Has been set up again.

The heart is a drum.
The drum has a snare.
The snare is in the blood.
The blood is in the air.

Listen to what they did.
Listen to what's to come.
Listen to the blood.
Listen to the drum.

The Ballad of the Imam and the Shah

An Old Persian Legend
to C. E. H.

It started with a stabbing at a well
Below the minarets of Isfahan.
The widow took her son to see them kill
The officer who'd murdered her old man.
The child looked up and saw the hangman's
    work –
The man who'd killed his father swinging high.
The mother said: 'My child, now be at peace.
The wolf has had the fruits of all his crime.'

From felony to felony to crime
From robbery to robbery to loss
From calumny to calumny to spite
From rivalry to rivalry to zeal

All this was many centuries ago –
The kind of thing that couldn't happen now –
When Persia was the empire of the Shah
And many were the furrows on his brow.
The peacock the symbol of his throne
And many were its jewels and its eyes
And many were the prisons in the land
And many were the torturers and spies.

From tyranny to tyranny to war
From dynasty to dynasty to hate
From villainy to villainy to death
From policy to policy to grave

The child grew up a clever sort of chap
And he became a mullah, like his dad –
Spent many years in exile and disgrace
Because he told the world the Shah was bad.
'Believe in God,' he said, 'believe in me.
Believe me when I tell you who I am.
Now chop the arm of wickedness away.
Hear what I say. I am the great Imam.'

From heresy to heresy to fire
From clerisy to clerisy to fear
From litany to litany to sword
From fallacy to fallacy to wrong

And so the Shah was forced to flee abroad.
The Imam was the ruler in his place.
He started ķilling everyone he could
To make up for the years of his disgrace.
And when there were no enemies at home
He sent his men to Babylon to fight.
And when he'd lost an army in that way
He knew what God was telling him was right.

From poverty to poverty to wrath
From agony to agony to doubt
From malady to malady to shame
From misery to misery to fight

He sent the little children out to war.
They went out with his portrait in their hands.
The desert and the marshes filled with blood.
The mothers heard the news in Isfahan.
Now Babylon is buried under dirt.
Persepolis is peeping through the sand.
The child who saw his father's killer killed
Has slaughtered half the children in the land.

From felony
to robbery
to calumny
to rivalry
to tyranny
to dynasty
to villainy
to policy
to heresy
to clerisy
to litany
to fallacy
to poverty
to agony
to malady
to misery –

The song is yours. Arrange it as you will.
Remember where each word fits in the line
And every combination will be true
And every permutation will be fine:

From policy to felony to fear
From litany to heresy to fire
From villainy to tyranny to war
From tyranny to dynasty to shame

From poverty to malady to grave
From malady to agony to spite
From agony to misery to hate
From misery to policy to fight!

I Saw a Child

I saw a child with silver hair.
Stick with me and I'll take you there.
    Clutch my hand.
    Don't let go.
The fields are mined and the wind blows cold.
The wind blows through his silver hair.

The Blue Vein River is broad and deep.
The branches creak and the shadows leap.
    Clutch my hand.
    Stick to the path.
The fields are mined and the moon is bright.
I saw a child who will never sleep.

Far from the wisdom of the brain
I saw a child grow old in pain.
    Clutch my hand.
    Stay with me.
The fields are mined by the enemy.
Tell me we may be friends again.

Far from the wisdom of the blood
I saw a child reach from the mud.
    Clutch my hand.
    Clutch my heart.
The fields are mined and the moon is dark.
The Blue Vein River is in full flood.

Far from the wisdom of the heart
I saw a child being torn apart.
    Is this you?
    Is this me?
The fields are mined and the night is long.
Stick with me when the shooting starts.

Tiananmen

Tiananmen
Is broad and clean
And you can't tell
Where the dead have been
And you can't tell
What happened then
And you can't speak
Of Tiananmen.

You must not speak.
You must not think.
You must not dip
Your brush in ink.
You must not say
What happened then,
What happened there
In Tiananmen.

The cruel men
Are old and deaf
Ready to kill
But short of breath
And they will die
Like other men
And they'll lie in state
In Tiananmen.

They lie in state.
They lie in style.
Another lie's
Thrown on the pile,
Thrown on the pile
By the cruel men
To cleanse the blood
From Tiananmen.

Truth is a secret.
Keep it dark.
Keep it dark
In your heart of hearts.
Keep it dark
Till you know when
Truth may return
To Tiananmen.

Tiananmen
Is broad and clean
And you can't tell
Where the dead have been
And you can't tell
When they'll come again.
They'll come again
To Tiananmen.

Hong Kong, June 15, 1989

The Ballad of the Shrieking Man

A shrieking man stood in the square
And he harangued the smart café
In which a bowlered codger sat
A-twirling of a fine moustache
A-drinking of a fine Tokay

And it was Monday and the town
Was working in a kind of peace
Excepting where the shrieking man
A-waving of his tattered limbs
Glared at the codger's trouser-crease

Saying

Coffee's mad
And tea is mad
And so are gums and teeth and lips.
The horror ships that ply the seas
The horror tongues that plough the teeth
The coat
The tie
The trouser clips
The purple sergeant with the bugger-grips
Will string you up with all their art
And laugh their socks off as you blow apart.

The codger seeming not to hear
Winked at the waiter, paid the bill
And walked the main street out of town
Beyond the school, beyond the works
Where the shrieking man pursued him still

And there the town beneath them lay
And there the desperate river ran.
The codger smiled a purple smile.
A finger sliced his waistcoat ope
And he rounded on the shrieking man

Saying

Tramps are mad
And truth is mad
And so are trees and trunks and tracks.
The horror maps have played us true.
The horror moon that slits the clouds
The gun
The goon
The burlap sacks
The purple waistcoats of the natterjacks
Have done their bit as you can see
To prise the madness from our sanity.

On Wednesday when the day was young
Two shrieking men came into town
And stopped before the smart café
In which another codger sat
Twirling his whiskers with a frown

And as they shrieked and slapped their knees
The codger's toes began to prance
Within the stitching of their caps
Which opened like a set of jaws
And forced him out to join the dance

Saying

Arms are mad
And legs are mad
And all the spaces in between.
The horror spleen that bursts its sack
The horror purple as it lunges through
The lung
The bung
The jumping-bean
The-I-think-you-know-what-you-think-I-mean
Are up in arms against the state
And all the body will disintegrate.

On Saturday the town was full
As people strolled in seeming peace
Until three shrieking men appeared
And danced before the smart café
And laughed and jeered and slapped their knees

And there a hundred codgers sat.
A hundred Adam's apples rose
And rubbed against their collar studs
Until the music came in thuds
And all the men were on their toes

Saying

Hearts are mad
And minds are mad
And bats are moons and moons are bats.
The horror cats that leap the tiles
The horror slates that catch the wind
The lice
The meat
The burning ghats
The children buried in the butter vats
The steeple crashing through the bedroom roof
Will be your answer if you need a proof.

The codgers poured into the square
And soon their song was on all lips
And all did dance and slap their knees
Until a horseman came in view –
The sergeant with the bugger-grips!

He drew his cutlass, held it high
And brought it down on hand and head
And ears were lopped and limbs were chopped
And still the sergeant slashed and slew
Until the codger crew lay dead

Saying

God is mad
And I am mad
And I am God and you are me.
The horror peace that boils the sight
The horror God turning out the light.
The Christ
Who killed
The medlar tree
Is planning much the same for you and me
And here's a taste of what's in store –
Come back again if you should want some more.

On Sunday as they hosed the streets
I went as usual to pray
And cooled my fingers at the stoup
And when the wafer touched my tongue
I thought about that fine Tokay

And so I crossed the empty square
And met the waiter with a wink
A-sweeping up of severed heads
A-piling up of bowler hats
And he muttered as he poured my drink

Saying

Waiting's mad
And stating's mad
And understating's mad as hell.
The undertakings we have made
The wonder breaking from the sky
The pin
The pen
The poisoned well
The purple sergeant with the nitrate smell
Have won their way and while we wait

The horror ships have passed the straits –
The vice
The vine
The strangler fig
The fault of thinking small and acting big
Have primed the bomb and pulled the pin
And we're all together when the roof falls in!

Fireflies of the Sea

Dip your hand in the water.
Watch the current shine.
See the blaze trail from your fingers,
Trail from your fingers,
Trail from mine.
There are fireflies on the island
And they cluster in one tree
And in the coral shallows
There are fireflies of the sea.

Look at the stars reflected
Now the sea is calm
And the phosphorus exploding,
Flashing like a starburst
When you stretch your arm.
When you reach down in the water
It's like reaching up to a tree,
To a tree clustered with fireflies,
Fireflies of the sea.

Dip your hand in the water.
Watch the current shine.
See the blaze trail from your fingers,
Trail from your fingers,
Trail from mine
As you reach down in the water,
As you turn away from me,
As you gaze down at the coral
And the fireflies of the sea.

Cut-Throat Christ

or the New Ballad of the Dosi Pares

Oh the Emperor sat on an ivory throne
And his wives were fat and all their jewels shone
And the Emperor said: It's plain to see
Christ was an emperor just like me.

Well the rich have a Christ and he's nobody's fool
And he pays for their kids to go to convent school
And their momma drives them home to tea.
She says: Christ is a rich bitch just like me.

But *I* say:

I say he sold his body to some foreign queer
And he sold his blood for just a case of beer
And he sold his soul to the fraternity.
Christ became a cut-throat just like me.

There's a Christ for a whore and a Christ for a punk
A Christ for a pickpocket and a drunk
There's a Christ for every sinner but one thing there aint –
There aint no Christ for any cutprice saint.

Well I was casting for fish by the North Harbour Pier
When this guy called Jesus says to me: Come here –
If you want to join the fraternity,
Lay down your nets and you can follow me.

So I left my nets and I left my line
And I followed my Jesus to the Quiapo shrine
And he told me many stories of his enemy –
It was General Ching of the EPD.

And I swore to the Black Nazarene there and then
I'd go out and kill one of the General's men
And when I brought my *beinte-nuebe* for the boss to see
That guy called Jesus he was proud of me.

Oh the Emperor sat on an ivory throne.
He had twelve brave peers and he loved each one.
We were twelve disciples and our strength was proved
But I was the disciple whom Jesus loved.

There's a Christ for a whore and a Christ for a punk
A Christ for a pickpocket and a drunk
There's a Christ for every sinner but one thing there aint –
There aint no Christ for any cutprice saint.

Well Jesus was a drinker as you might expect.
We got through plenty stainless and a few long necks
And then Jesus got mad as mad can be.
He said: One of you punks is gonna squeal on me.

Now that General Ching has put a price on my head
With disciples like you I'm as good as dead –
There's one who will betray me to the EPD.
We said: Tell me boss, tell me boss, is it me?

But there wasn't the leisure and there wasn't the time
To find out from Jesus who would do this crime
For a shot rang out and we had to flee
From General Ching and half the military.

Oh the Emperor sat on an ivory throne
And out of twelve brave peers there was just one bad one
And Christ had twelve disciples and they loved him so
But one out of twelve is just the way things go.

There's a Christ for a whore and a Christ for a punk
A Christ for a pickpocket and a drunk
There's a Christ for every sinner but one thing there aint –
There aint no Christ for any cutprice saint.

Well I ran like crazy and I ran like fuck
And for the next three days I did my best to duck
And then I made my way back to the EPD.
I said: The General said he had a job for me.

Well the General he saw me and his face grew grim.
He said: Watch it guys, don't stand too close to him –
That's our old friend Judas and he wants his fee,
But the guy called Jesus he is roaming free.

I said: What's the deal? He said: We killed him, sure,
We filled him full of what we had and then some more,
We dumped him back in Tondo for his momma to see
And now he's resurrected with a one, two, three.

I said: General Ching, if what you say is true
I'm gonna need some protection out of you.
He said: Just pay him off now and let me be –
We don't protect a mediocrity.

'Cos the Emperor sat on an ivory throne
But that was long ago and now the Emperor's gone
And this guy called Jesus he is something new:
You crucify him once and he comes back for you.

We've dumped him in the Pasig, we've thrown him
    in the Bay,
We've nixed him in the cogon by the Superhighway,
We've chopped him into pieces and we've spread him
    around
But three days later he is safe and he is sound.

There's a Christ for a whore and a Christ for a punk
A Christ for a pickpocket and a drunk
There's a Christ for every sinner but one thing there aint –
There aint no Christ for any cutprice saint.

Now Manila's not the place for a defenceless thing –
You either go with Jesus or with General Ching
And I'd been with both and after what I'd been
I knew my only hope was the Black Nazarene.

So I go barefoot down to Quiapo and the streets are
    packed
And they're carrying the Nazarene on their backs
And just one step and it's plain to see
That Christ will crush them to eternity –

The Christ of the Aztecs, the Juggernaut God,
The Christ of the Thorn and the Christ of the Rod
And they're carrying the Christ along two lengths of rope
'Cos the Cut-Throat Christ's a cut-throat's only hope

And there's the man who killed the Carmelites, the
    Tad-tad gang,
The man who sells the ArmaLites in Alabang
And General Ching, the EPD, the senatorial bets,
The twelve disciples and the drum majorettes,

The Emperor Charlemagne, the rich bitch and the queer,
The guy called Jesus by the North Harbour Pier
And they're coming down to Quiapo and they've all made
    a vow
To wipe the sweat from the Black Nazarene's brow.

Oh the Emperor sat on an ivory throne
But in a cut-throat world a man is on his own
And what I've got is what you see –
Cut-Throat Christ, don't turn your back on me.

Gabriel

I come home to the cottage.
I climb the balcony.
It's the archangel Gabriel
Waiting there for me.

He says: Boss, boss, cut the loss,
Don't take on so.
Don't get mad with Gabriel.
Let it go.

I go into the kitchen
To fix myself a drink.
It's the archangel Gabriel
Weeping by the sink.

He says: Boss, boss, cut the loss,
Don't take on so.
Don't get mad with Gabriel.
Let it go.

I say: You've been away in Magsaysay,
You've not clocked in all week;
You're as strong as an ox,
But you're work-shy
With your head bowed low and your
    pleading eyes
And I'm too mad to speak.

I come home two hours later.
The archangel drops a tear.
He's sitting there in the same old chair
And he's drunk all the beer.

He says: Boss, boss, cut the loss,
Don't take on so.
Don't get mad with Gabriel.
Let it go.

I say: You've drunk yourself into outer space.
You're giving me one of those looks.
You're as wild as the moon in storm time
And I'd like to know the reason I'm
Supposed to keep you on the books.

Yes I should have known when I took you on
When you tumbled from the sky
That you're set in your ways and that's all.
You're a Gabriel and you've had a fall.
You can't change and nor can I
Gabriel
You can't change and nor can I.

The Ballad of the Birds

There's a mynah bird a-squawking
In the ipil-ipil tree.
I say: What do you want,
What do you want,
What do you want from me?
For my crops have all been planted
And the rainy season's here
But the baby in the hammock
Will not see out the year

And it goes

Crack crack
I'll be back
I'll be back like a heart attack
I'll be back when your hopes are wrecked
I'll be back when you most expect

There's a turtle dove a-weeping
In the crest of the dap-dap tree.
I say: What do you want,
What do you want,
What do you want from me?
For my son has gone to Saudi
And my daughter's in the States
But I'll have to borrow money
And I can't afford the rate

And it goes

Coo coo
Hard on you
Crack crack
I'll be back
I'll be back like a heart attack
I'll be back when your hopes are wrecked
I'll be back when you most expect

And the kingfisher goes shrieking
At the edge of the shining sea.
I say: What do you want,
What do you want,
What do you want from me?
For my wife has gone to the graveyard
To clear the weeds away
And the rains have failed and the land is dry
And there'll be some grief today

And it goes

Kraa kraa
Life is hard
Coo coo
Hard on you
Crack crack
I'll be back
I'll be back like a heart attack
I'll be back when your hopes are wrecked
I'll be back when you most expect

There are sparrows in the paddy
On the road to the cemetery.
I say: What do you want,
What do you want,
What do you want from me?
There's a grief that knocks you senseless.
There's a grief that drives you wild.
It picks you up.
It throws you down.
It grabs your hair.
It throws you in the air.
At the coffin of a child

And it goes

Peep peep
A child comes cheap
Kraa kraa
Life is hard
Coo coo
Hard on you
Crack crack
I'll be back
I'll be back like a heart attack
I'll be back when your hopes are wrecked
I'll be back when you most expect

Oh I'm nothing but a farmer
In the harvest of the year
And the rains have failed
And the land is sold
And I'm left in grief and fear
And there's a carrion crow alighting
On the crest of the banyan tree.
I say: What do you want,
What do you want,
What in the name of God do you want
    from me?

I Know What I'm Missing

It's a birdcall from the treeline.
I hear it every day.
It's the loveliest of the songbirds
And I'm glad it comes this way
And I stop to listen
And forget what I've to do
And I know what I'm missing –
My friend
My friend.

It's fluttering in the palm fronds
With a flash of black and gold.
It's the whistling of the oriole
And its beauty turns me cold
And I stop to listen
And forget what I've to do
And I know what I'm missing –
My friend
My friend.

Do you wonder if I'll remember?
Do you wonder where I'll be?
I'll be home again next winter
And I hope you'll write to me.
When the branches glisten
And the frost is on the avenue
I'll know what I'm missing –
My friend
My friend
I'm missing you.

Here Come the Drum Majorettes!

There's a girl with a fist full of fingers.
There's a man with a fist full of fivers.
There's a thrill in a step as it lingers.
There's a chance for a pair of salivas –

For the

Same hat
Same shoes
Same giddy widow on a sunshine cruise
Same deck
Same time
Same disappointment in a gin-and-lime

It's the same chalk on the blackboard!
It's the same cheese on the sideboard!
It's the same cat on the boardwalk!
It's the same broad on the catwalk!

There's a Gleb on a steppe in a dacha.
There's a Glob on a dig on the slack side.
There's a Glubb in the sand (he's a pasha).
There's a glib gammaglob in your backside

Saying

Gleb meet Glubb.
Glubb meet Glob.
God that's glum, that glib Glob dig.
'Dig that bog!'

'Frag that frog.'
'Stap that chap, he snuck that cig.'

It's the same ice on the racetrack!
It's the same track through the pack ice!
It's the same brick in the ice pack!
It's the same trick with an ice pick!

There's a thing you can pull with your eyeballs.
There's a tin you can pour for a bullshot.
There's a can you can shoot for a bullseye.
There's a man you can score who's an eyesore.

I'm an
Eyesore,
You're the thing itself.
You've a
Price or
You'd be on the shelf.
I'm a loner
In a lonesome town –
Barcelona –
It can get you down.

It's the same scare with a crowbar!
It's the same crow on the barstool!
It's the same stool for the scarecrow!
It's the same bar!

Ho!

Ha!

Like a spark from the stack of a liner
Like a twig in the hands of a dowser
With the force of the fist of a miner
(With the grace and the speed of a trouser)

In a

Blue moon
In a blue lagoon
She's got blue blue bloomers in a blue monsoon.

Wearing blue boots
And a blue zoot suit
He's a cruising bruiser with a shooter and a cute little
Twin blade
Sin trade
In a
Blue brown
New Town.

It's the same hand on the windpipe!
It's the same sand in the windsock!
It's the same brand on the handbag!
It's the same gland in the handjob!

The room is black.
The knuckles crack.
The blind masseuse walks up your back.
The saxophone
Is on its own
Pouring out the *Côtes du Rhône*.

When you're down to your last pair of piastres.
When you're down on your luck down in Przemyśl,
When your life is a chain of disasters
And your death you believe would be sameish,

When the goat has gone off with the gander
Or the goose with the grebe or the grouper
Then – a drum majorette – you can stand her:
She's a brick – she's a gas – she's a trouper

Saying

Jane meet John.
John meet Jane.
Take those jimjams off again
Jezebel.
Just as well.
Join the jive with Jules and June.
Geoffrey, Jesus, Jason, Jim,
Jenny, Jilly, Golly Gee –
If it's the same for you and him
It's the same for you and me:

It's the same grin on the loanshark!
It's the same goon in the sharkskin!
It's the same shark in the skin-game!
It's the same game
Same same

It's the same old rope for to skip with!
It's the same Old Nick for to sup with
   With a long spoon
   To the wrong tune

And it's hard for a heart to put up with!

The Orange Dove of Fiji

to R. & B. O'H.

On the slopes of Taveuni
The Barking Pigeons woof
But when I saw the Orange Dove
I nearly hit the roof

And would have surely had there been
A roof around to hit
But the roofs of Taveuni
Are down on the lower bit

While up there in the forest
The Silktails have survived
Where they 'forage in the substage'
And you feel you have *arrived*

As an amateur ornithologist
In the midst of a silktail flock
Until you hear behind you
A 'penetrating tock'

And you find six feet above your head
What you were looking for –
The Orange Dove of Fiji,
No less, no more.

The female of the Orange Dove
Is actually green.
The really orange *male* Orange Dove
Is the one you've seen.

It must have been dipped in Day-Glo
Held by its bright green head.
The colour is preposterous.
You want to drop down dead.

It turns around upon its perch
Displaying all the bits
That are mentioned in Dick Watling's book
And the description fits.

Then it says: 'Tock – okay, is that
Enough to convince you yet?
Because that, my friend, is all tock tock
That you are going to get.'

Oh the Many-Coloured Fruit Dove
Is pretty enough to boot
And I'm afraid the purple swamphen
Looks queerer than a coot

Like a flagrant English Bishop
Let loose among his flock
With brand-new orange gaiters
(And that's just the swamphen cock)

But the Orange Dove is something
Spectacular to see
So I hope they don't fell another single
Taveuni tree.

The Manila Manifesto

Nagdadaláng takot, hiya't alang-alang
nag-aalapaap yaring gunam-gunam
mapuról na noo at dilang mabagal
iwaksí ang takot at kapanganiban.

Sa actualmenteng aking pagkatayo
indecibleng tuwa'y kinamtang ng puso
saan mangagaling at saan hahango
sabing conveniente sa tanáng pinuno.

Pupunuan ko na yaring sasabihin
anhin ang maraming kuntil-butil
di raw mahahapay kahoy na puputlin
kung yamba nang yamba't di tuluyang tagin.

What you need for poetry is a body and a voice. It doesn't have to be a great body or a great voice. But it ought ideally to be *your* body, and it ought to be *your* voice.

The parent helps the child discover what may be done with its lips and its limbs. This is the first poetry.

A sort of night then falls – a melancholy mercy – after which the initiation is mysteriously forgotten. This is the primal erasure.

The remainder of our lives is spent in recapturing that initial sense of discovery. This is the second poetry.

But the wisdom of the age has forbidden us the use of our lips and our limbs. This wisdom is the enemy of poetry.

You call yourself a poet?
Don't you see, you're incomplete
With your double-nelson plaster cast
And your disenfranchised feet?

¶

In Madame Vendler's Chamber of Horrors I saw seven
American poets, strung up by their swaddling-bands
     and crying: More Pap! More Pap!

¶

A foreign body
Dug up in Manila
In a state of advanced decay
Turned out to be that
Of Theophilus Pratt
Who resumes supervision today
In L.A.

I saw seven beautiful women, the dreaded Manananggal
of Atimonan, who, as I approached, arose and flapped
away and I perceived they had left behind the lower
part of their bodies. 'Mga Manananggal, Mga
Manananggal,' I cried after them, 'saan ang punta.'
They hung momently in the flowering crest of the
Dapdap tree. 'Pupunta kami sa IOWA, pare ko,'
laughed one, and they clattered off over the Pacific.

Prayer

'Lord, give me back my body
And give me back my voice.'
'Son, I would give your body back
But alas I have no choice.

'For you have pawned your arms and legs,
Your fingers and your toes
And you sold your voice to the bottle-boy
For twenty-one pesos.'

'Oh Lord, redeem my pawn-ticket
And find that bottle-boy too.'
'Your ticket, son, has passed its date
And your body is glue

'And the bottle-boy has pushed his cart
Back home to his Tondo slum
And the Sigue-Sigue Sputnik gang
They laughed to see him come

'And they snatched away your voice from him
For he sang so tunefully
And they slit the throat of the bottle-boy
And they threw him in the sea

'And they passed your voice from hand to hand
And your song was in their mouth
And they went to war with the Tad-tad gang
And the Ativan gang
In Alabang
By the Superhighway South.

'For seven days and seven nights
Your voice rose o'er the fray
And you would tremble had you heard
The things I heard you say.'

I saw Emily Dickinson in a vision and asked if it was merely by coincidence that so much of her poetry could be sung to the tune of 'The Yellow Rose of Texas'. She said: 'In poetry there is no coincidence. I had feet once. I had knees. I would not have you think I had no knees.'

¶

Pain like the Flemish!
Give weight to the blemish!

Down with a cautious perfection!
Down with a bloodless circumspection!

So you despise my fecklessness?
I pity your lack of recklessness.

This is the new fearlessness.
That is the old earlessness.

This is the new recklessness.
That is the old what-the-hecklessness.

Voici la Nouvelle Insouciance.
Voilà . . . hein?

Die Neue Rücksichtlosigkeit –
I would pronounce it if I might
Von Ewigkeit bis Ewigkeit –
Die Neue Rücksichtlosigkeit.

.

An arrow was shot from Teheran. A novelist lifted a shield. A thousand arrows were shot from Boston. A thousand poets died.

¶

We call on America to stop killing, torturing and imprisoning its poets.

¶

Sa Kusina

Ako'y Pilipino
Pili at pipino
Sili, luya
At sibuyas –
Ako'y Pilipino.

Blank terror doth stalk
The poets of New York.

¶

The Exchange

I met the Muse of Censorship
And she had packed her bags
And all the folk of Moscow
Were hanging out the flags.

I asked her what her prospects were
And whither her thoughts did range.
She said: 'I am off to Dublin town
On a cultural exchange.

'And folk there be in Cambridge
Who like the way I think
And there be folk in Nottingham
Whom I shall drown in ink

'And when we reach America
The majorettes will sing:
Here comes the Muse of Censorship –
This is a very good thing.'

I went to the Finland Station
To wave the Muse goodbye
And on another platform
A crowd I did espy.

I saw the Muse of Freedom
Alighting from the train.
Far from that crowd I wept aloud
For to see that Muse again.

The Approval

You tell me that your poems
Have been approved in France.
Well, that settles that!
Or aren't you ashamed, perchance

To cite this recognition
On the grounds that it's French.
What language do you feel in?
You make me blench.

This is no time for people who say: this, this, and only this. We say: this, and *this,* and *that* too.

¶

An Amazing Dialogue

'But this poem is not like that poem!'
'No, you are right, it's not.'

The Poetry of Pure Fact

One prawn
with an ablated eye
can spawn
as many as one million fry.

We despise terrorist normative critics.

¶

We despise the deformed, uncandid class-consciousness
of our domestic criticism. On our map, there are no
compass points. North, for instance, does not mean good.

¶

We say to France: AUT TACE AUT LOQUERE
MELIORA SILENTIO – either shut up or say
something worth saying.

A Poem against Barn Owls

Some people think that barn owls
are an endangered species
but they are found all round the world
as are their faeces.

The Gene-Pool

Get out of the gene-pool, Gene,
And take your tambourine.
You write the way you speak.
You're not one of our clique.
You say the things you mean.
Out of the gene-pool, Gene.

Get out of the gene-pool, Gene,
And go behind that screen.
You don't respect our style.
You sometimes crack a smile.
Your insouciance is obscene.
Out of the gene-pool, Gene.

You don't belong to our age.
You don't 'write for the page'.
You put us in a rage.
You are unclean!
Get out! Get out!
Out of the gene-pool, Gene.

An Indistinct Inscription Near Kom Omho
(Meroitic Cursive)

I was born to a kiss and a smile,
I was born to the hopes of a prince,
I dipped my pen in the Nile
And it hasn't functioned since.

The Answer

'Stop! Stop! Stop!
Stop in your tracks.
Because you are not with us
You are holding everyone back.'

'Friend, you and your friends go your way
And I'll go mine.
I've enough water to survive
But far too little wine.'

(Crocodilopolis Papyrus no. 10743)

RECENT WORK

At the Kerb
i.m. Mick Imlah

Grief to bestow, where once they bestowed their beauty,
Who are these mourners processing to the grave,
Each bearing a history like a precious ointment
And tender on their sleeves the wounds of love?

Brutal disease has numbered him a victim,
As if some unmarked car had appeared one day
And snatched him off to torture and confinement,
Then dumped him by the kerbside and sped away;

As if they stooped now at the kerb to lift the body,
As if they broke the jars and the unguent flowed,
Flowed down the sleeves and wounds, ran down the
    kerbstones,
Grief to bestow what beauty once bestowed.

Yellow Tulips

Looking into the vase, into the calyx, into the water drop,
Looking into the throat of the flower at the pollen stain,
I can see the ambush love sprung once in the summery
    wood,
I can see the casualties where they lay, till they set forth
    again.

I can see the lips, parted first in surprise, parted in desire,
Smile now as the silence falls on the yellow-dappled ride
For each thinks the other can hear each receding thought
On each receding tide.

They have come out of the wood now. They are skirting
    the fields
Between the tall wheat and the hedge, on the unploughed
    strips,
And they believe anyone who saw them would know
Every secret of their limbs and of their lips,

As if, like creatures of legend, they had come down out
    of the mist
Back to their native city and stood in the square,
And they were seen to be marked at the throat with a
    certain sign
Whose meaning all could share.

These flowers came from a shop. Really they looked
    nothing much
Till they opened as if in surprise at the heat of this hotel.
Then the surprise turned to a shout, and the girl said,
    'Shall I chuck them now
Or give them one more day? They've not lasted so well.'

'Oh give them one more day. They've lasted well enough.
They've lasted as love lasts, which is longer than most
    maintain.
Look at the sign it has left here at the throat of the flower
And on your tablecloth – look at the pollen stain.'

Memorial

We spoke, we chose to speak of war and strife –
  A task a fine ambition sought –
And some might say, who shared our work, our life:
  That praise was dearly bought.

Drivers, interpreters, these were our friends.
  These we loved. These we were trusted by.
The shocked hand wipes the blood across the lens.
  The lens looks to the sky.

Most died by mischance. Some seemed honour-bound
  To take the lonely, peerless track
Conceiving danger as a testing-ground
  To which they must go back

Till the dry tongue fell silent and they crossed
  Beyond the realm of time and fear.
Death waved them through the checkpoint. They were lost.
  All have their story here.

The Twister

That was one hot day.
The music refused to play.
The hay lay in lines in the fields,
Grey in the sun,
And there was nothing useful to be done.

Then came a little twister in the heat,
Lifted the hay and dropped it in the lane
And all along the village street.
The dry grass hung from the power lines
Like music from a music sheet.

As if some genius had defaced the staves
With long limp slurs and semiquaver tails
Which fell from the power lines as the day died
And came to rest among the graves
Leaving a clean sheet, leaving nothing to play.

That was one hot day.
All the musicians had gone away
And I had time and music on my hands,
Folding away the music stands
And throwing out one dry forgotten bouquet.

No one was there.
The music hung in the air
Like a soft mockery dropping through the day.

Let's Go Over It All Again

. . . Some people are like that.
They split up and then they think:
 Hey, maybe we haven't hurt each other to
   the uttermost.
Let's meet up and have a drink.

Let's go over it all again.
Let's rake over the dirt.
Let me pick that scab of yours.
Does it hurt.

Let's go over what went wrong –
How and why and when.
Let's go over what went wrong
Again and again.

We hurt each other badly once.
We said a lot of nasty stuff.
But lately I've been thinking how
I didn't hurt you enough.

Maybe there's more where that came from,
Something more malign.
Let me damage you again
For auld lang syne.
Yes, let me see you bleed again
For auld lang syne.

The Vapour Trail

Now through the grating of my cell
I look up at a strip of autumn sky
And often, chalked across the blue,
There's a vapour trail,
A vapour trail . . .
And then, I don't know why,
My dear friend,
I start to think of you.

Dawn brings these planes from distant lands,
Red-eyed tycoons from far-flung ports of call.
Dawn lifts the luggage through the flaps
Onto the carousel
The carousel
And wakes the baggage hall.
Dawn will bring you, perhaps.

Perhaps that vapour trail is where
Your plane passed over me here in my jail.
That line is the trajectory
Of your breakfast tray
Your breakfast tray.
Perhaps that is your trail
And you look down on me.

Look down on me, my friend, look down
And think of me now as I think of you
And think of us as we were then
From your vapour trail,
Your vapour trail . . .
Your line of chalk on blue.
Think well of me again,
    My friend –
    Whatever hurt I may have done,
    For I intended none.
    Forgive the hurt that I did not intend
    And let it mend.
Think well of me again.

The Alibi

My mind was racing.
It was some years from now.
We were together again in our old flat.
You were admiring yourself adjusting your hat.
'Oh of course I was mad then,' you said with a
   forgiving smile,
'Something snapped in me and I was mad for a while.'

But this madness of yours disgusted me,
This alibi,
This gorgeous madness like a tinkling sleigh,
It carried you away
Snug in your fur, snug in your muff and cape.
You made your escape
Through the night, over the dry powdery snow.
I watched you go.

Truly the mad deserve our sympathy.
And you were driven mad you said by me
And then you drove away,
The cushions and the furs piled high,
Snug with your madness alibi,
Injured and forgiven on your loaded sleigh.

Spanish Songs

1. The Soldier Limping Down the Track

The soldier limping down the track,
The pilgrim at the inn,
Each bears a story on his back.
Each has a yarn to spin.

One travels with a seething heart.
One comes from fearful wars.
Give them some wine. They'll show their wounds
By firelight, by the stars.

They talk the blazing night away
And the wine suits them well.
They never ask a thing of me.
I have no tale to tell.

South by the stars lies Africa.
North lie the lands that freeze.
I never trod those frozen roads
Nor crossed those boiling seas.

They talk the blazing night away.
I listen as I lie.
The moon looks down and laughs at me
And the stars burn in the sky.
The moon sticks out its tongue at me
And the stars burn in the sky.

2. The Ballad of the Raven

Oh take the arrow from your bow.
Point it not to the sky.
For the raven is a royal bird.
King Arthur did not die.
The raven is a royal bird.
King Arthur did not die.

The King was charmed by Merlin's art
When his heart broke for woe.
King Arthur flew from Camelot,
A raven black as the sloe.
He cried as he flew from Camelot,
A raven black as the sloe.

The King flew from the English land
Until he came to a plain.
He saw a knight beneath a tree
Under the sun of Spain.
The knight lay asleep beneath a tree
Under the sun of Spain.

Look up, look up, Sir Lancelot
Look up into the tree.
I Arthur am, your raven king
And you were false to me
Your raven king, your royal friend
And you were false to me.

I am not dead, the raven said,
I shall be King again.
But you shall die beneath the sky
Under the sun of Spain.
False you shall die beneath the sky
Under the sun of Spain.

3. The Watching Man

I wake at night with a start.
A log slides from the grate.
And what was that? A cat? A rat?
I hate them both with all my heart.
What business have they being up so late?

And what about that man
On the dark side of the square?
What harm has he in mind for me?
What reckoning? What plan?
What purpose has he standing watching there?

The night is on the tiles.
A mood settles on the moon.
It gives the wateriest of all watery smiles.
It will be gone soon.

But when the smile is gone
And darkness has its day
The watcher below my window will watch on.
He will not slip away.

The lovers hurry by
The watcher in the square.
They seem so busy with their ecstasy.
Hatred has time to spare.

Hatred knows no land,
No hearth, no wife, no brood,
And time lies easy on the hater's hand
And cold as the moon's mood.

Though I take the forest track
Or climb the mountain trail
I'll never shake the hatred off my back,
The watcher off my tail.

In the stable lantern's soot,
In the soft step on the stair,
I shall catch the eye, I shall waken to the foot
Of the watcher in the square.

4. Oh Run to the Door

Oh run to the door, mother, run to the door
And look in the eyes of your son
And bid me farewell as they take me away
And forgive me for what I have done
And watch till I come to the dip in the road
And forgive me for what I have done.

Oh run from the fell, brother, run from the fell
And call the flock down to the fold
And comfort your mother and be with her now
In the room where your father lies cold
And be with her now through the heat of the night
In the room where your father lies cold.

They have taken the vinegar sponge to his head,
They have wrung out his blood in a bowl.
Let them wash all the hatred from out of his heart.
Let them wring out the bile from his soul.
Let them wash all the bitterness out of his heart
And the vengefulness out of his soul.

There's a ship in the bay in the heat of the day.
There's a bench that is waiting for me.
And the law of the ship is the chain and the whip,
The chain and the whip and the sea.
I am bound by the law to the chain and the whip.
I am chained by the law to the sea.

Oh run to the door mother, run to the door
And look in the eyes of your son.
I am dead, I am dead as the father I killed.
Forgive me for what I have done.
I am bound by a chain to the ship of the dead.
O mother forgive your dead son.

5. Wake Now

Where are you making for? O troubled soul,
    I heard you call in your sleep.
I saw you strike out at some pestering foe.
    Some hand was dragging you,
Some hand was dragging you down into the deep.

Was it a river bank? Was it a shore?
    You seemed to halt in your quest
And I was afraid to shake you awake before
    You had fought off that hand,
You had fought off that hand and won your rest.

I see you have won it now. I was afraid.
    They say men meet death in their dreams
And they must be left alone to fight that shade,
    Fight on that lonely shore
Fight on that lonely shore and by those streams.

I see you stir. I see you are riding back
    As if you were coming home on leave
Carrying Death's written bargain in your pack
    And living were nothing more
And living were nothing more than a brave reprieve.

    Wake now and welcome home.
Wake now and welcome home to that reprieve.

6. The Night Comes Down Like a Cloak

The night comes down like a cloak.
The light is gone in the West.
The sheep are still in the fold.
My love lies asleep on my breast.
Sleep on, my love, sleep on.
Your child wakes in my womb.
Come sunrise you'll be gone.

Oh he loved me more in the dark
Than ever he did in the day.
I dare not stir for the fear
When he wakes he will up and away.
Sleep on my love, sleep on.
Your child wakes in my womb.
Come sunrise you'll be gone.

For love belongs to the night
As the wolf belongs to the hill.
A man may move in the dark
As a fox moves in for the kill.

A kiss can stifle a cry.
A mouth can smother a breath.
Love can ruin a life.
Love makes a gift of a death.

Love can ruin a life
As a crop can ruin a tree.
This child of yours that I bear
Will be the death of me.

You will wash your face at the well.
You will turn your brow to the South.
I shall taste the last of your smile
In the brisk farewell of your mouth.
Sleep on, my love, sleep on.
Your child wakes in my womb.

    The child wakes.
    The branch breaks.
Come sunrise you'll be gone.

7. I Was Born with a Stain on My Chin

I was born with a stain on my chin.
I was born to the stench of a sty.
My mother said Son you were fathered in sin.
My father said Boy you were born in a bin
And you'd better get used to the mess you are in.
Look at life through a sow-gelder's eye –
      Good or bad –
Look at life through a sow-gelder's eye.

So they taught me the sow-gelder's art
And they set me to work with the swine
At a simple procedure involving a part
Where a single incision is certain to smart.
When it comes to pursuing affairs of the heart
I'm just glad that they left me with mine –
      Good or bad –
I'm glad that they left me with mine.

Well they left me with more than enough
As many a lover has found.
Though my manner is bluff and my methods are tough,
If a girl has the time and the taste for the rough,
I'm endowed with a ready supply of the stuff
And I'm happy to share it around –
      Good or bad –
I'm delighted to spread it around.

When the women come out on the street
At the sound of the sow-gelder's horn
And I see something sharp in the eyes that I greet
And I drop them a word they would blush to repeat
And they mention a place and a time we could meet,
Should I wish that I'd never been born? –
        Good or bad –
Should I wish that I'd never been born?

I was born with a stain on my chin.
I was born to the stench of a sty.
My mother said Son you were fathered in sin.
My father said Boy you were born in a bin
And you'd better get used to the mess you are in.
Look at life through a sow-gelder's eye –
        Good or bad –
Look at life through a sow-gelder's eye.

Martine's Song

Write a letter to the dead.
Write to for the dead to read.
Oh the dead have swum too far.
They have swum beyond the sea.

Take the letter in your hand.
Make a fold, and make a fold.
Fold it into a little boat
And place a candle in the hold.

Let the paper boat float on
Where the river meets the sea.
That is where my heart belongs.
That is where I want to be.

Every candle is a star.
Every boat floats out to sea –
Which I think is not too far
And that is where I long to be.

And that is where I long to be.

Cosmology

We know where the cauldrons were buried
And the axes, the flesh-hooks and the spits.
We know the site of the obsidian mines and the source of the
    chocolate flint.
But who put these questions first we will never know.

Who noticed the Sun rise in winter between the Wolf's Teeth
And thought to mark the summer's trajectory?
Who measured the shadow?
Who sank the great pits for the calendar stones?
Who kept in mind an ancient calculation
And served his tribe for a memory?

We know that the stars were constant to the navigator's eye
But who first remarked the planets in their retrograde motions,
Who first saw the sky as a question – that we do not know –
Or who first conceived the Earth as a general proposition.

When the season favoured the ships and the horizons were
    friendly,
When wind and current carried men forth like a desire,
And the village rounded on the young: 'Be gone, or be a
    burden to us,'
They found the old tales to be true, of land succeeding to land
And life beyond the promontory, places of distant wealth.

But who first thought of the moon as a place
In the sense that an archipelago is a place?
Who saw this place pass overhead?
Who viewed the sky as an archipelago
And the constellations as a clock?
Who enrolled in the night as in a university
And abandoned the archipelago,
Vanishing into the breakers one summer evening
Dedicating his destiny to the spheres?

We have marked the first lands to be beggared by tillage
And the epoch when sheep first yielded wool,
We can question the composition of a tooth,
We can fix the age of a splinter.
We are renowned for our superb equations.

But the music is lost that served the oarsmen for a metre
And the songs are forgotten that praised the Moon and
    the Sun
For the fourteen divisions of summer
While the winter months went nameless and unsung.

They built their ships not from a drawn design
But by a series of learned procedures.
They sang their boats into being.
They sang what they knew of the skies
And they sang the names of every visible star.

But who first said where I walk is Earth
And where I drown is Earth as well –
My hearth as a man, my roof-tree, my harbour, my grave?
Who first saw the Moon as an Earth at a distance?

All the evidence was destined to be lost –
Every chanted word, every sketch in the sand,
All thoughts committed to leaf and skin –
And this largest thought, this first cosmologist
Must have grasped for an instant before shying away from it,
Pushing it away from him to wait
As these questions have waited for their tens of thousands
    of seasons,
Patient or indifferent to our expertise.

Rain

The sweet rain falls on the sea
Far from the land.
They stretch a torn sail taut between torn hands
To fill the pail.
They turn their channelled faces to the sky
And the sweet rain runs in their eyes
And on the channelled sea.